Tech Survival 101

Greg Jensen and Tom Henricksen

Other Books from Tom Henricksen:

Explore IT: Helping you understand your options in technology

TechnoLeaders

Pursuing IT

Relationship Management for Technical Professionals

Copyright © 2019 Greg Jensen and Tom Henricksen.

All rights reserved. No portion of this book may be reproduced in any form without permission from the publisher, except as permitted by U.S. copyright law.

For permissions, contact: Tom Henricksen (515) 333-1255, tom@myitcareercoach.com

First Edition

Contents

Part I – Introduction to the Technology Field 1

    How Does Technology Work in an Organization? 2

    IT Titles, Departments, and More 6

    Finding the Right Fit for You 11

    More than a Paycheck: Salary and Benefits 15

Part II - Operation and Engineering Issues 19

    Understanding Business Stakeholders 20

    Common Engineer Issues 24

    Operations and Security Pitfalls 28

    Programmers Be Crazy! 32

Part III - Assets and Branding 35

    It Is Great to Be Here! 36

    Your Most Valuable Assets 39

    Building Your Personal Brand 42

    It Is All in the Performance 46

    Your Online Brand with LinkedIn 50

    Branding Through the Community 53

Part IV - Mindset and Culture 57

    Participate and Share 58

Permission to Succeed 62

Don't Be Bashful, Just Ask! 65

Evolving Your Mindset 68

Developing Your Own Tech Radar 71

Defining Your Core Values 74

What Do I Look for in Culture? 78

Are You Looking for Abundance or Scarcity? 81

Are You Real or an Impostor? 84

Staying Above the Line: Drama or Presence 87

Part V - Leadership 91

Stepping to the Front 92

Leader Performance = Team Performance 95

Building a Great Tech Team 98

Part I – Introduction to the Technology Field

How Does Technology Work in an Organization?

As you start your career in technology, you might wonder about the big picture. How do all the pieces work together? What does the chief information officer (CIO) do? How does the chief technology officer (CTO) fit into the picture? Depending on which level you enter into the technology organization, you may have different vantage points. My first role was as a programmer/analyst at a small consulting firm. Each organization does things a little differently. Overall though, they have some similarities.

C-Suite

The leaders of an organization are commonly referred to as the C-suite or executives. This includes the chief executive officer or CEO, the person in charge of everything and who answers to ownership or the board. The chief information officer is responsible for the technology team or Information Services and sets the tone on policies and procedures and helps drive major initiatives. Some organizations have a chief technology officer. Executives in this role set high-level technology operations. The CIO and CTO often work together on overall technology strategy. The chief operating officer or COO is responsible for day to day operations of the company. Depending on the business field the organization is in, they may also have a chief security officer. This person is responsible for enforcing policies and procedures that ensure security breaches do not occur.

VPs and Directors

The next level below is for the vice president. Some companies will include executive and senior vice presidents, too. This is usually the case for larger organizations. Further down the leadership hierarchy, decisions transition from more strategic to more tactical, day-to-day operations. Some leaders, as they move up the ladder, still appear to keep their heads 'in the weeds' of the day to day, i.e., immersed or preoccupied with the details. Directors are at the next level down and usually have multiple managers reporting to them. The technology team may have a director of software development, director of infrastructure, and directory of security. The responsibilities can vary quite a bit for each organization.

Architects and Engineers

Architects in the technology sector generally lay down high-level plans similar to their distant occupational relatives who create plans for buildings. Architects can be found in software design, infrastructure, networks, and a few other areas. Engineers work alongside the architects to put the plans into practice. For example, the software architect creates the design and the software engineers write the code. There is usually a lot of collaboration between these two areas.

Managers

Managers are at the lowest management rung. They work in the day-to-day operations exclusively. Team sizes may vary but often the number of employees who report directly to a manager is five to ten. As a former manager of software development, up to ten people reported to me an any given time. If you enjoy developing people, this is a great level to be at. Expect to have ample opportunity to lead a team and help people.

Analysts

When I first started out of college, I was a programmer/analyst. I thought my title was odd since I mostly developed or programmed software. Although, I got the chance to do more analysis at various points during my first job. For my next job, I worked with a larger organization. They had people who only did the analysis. Analysts wrote up requirements and shared them with a developer to complete. Some companies call them systems analysts or business analysts but overall, they are responsible for generating requirements.

Titles

From organization to organization, titles can change quite a bit. For instance, some places have numerous designations for the same thing. They might use titles, such as Programmer Intern, Programmer I, Programmer II, etc. It can be difficult to compare titles when considering opportunities or resumes. It is more helpful to ask someone what they do or what roles someone in that position would have. This can make salary comparison difficult as well.

Structure

Organizations use many different structures. Some still have a hierarchy similar to that of a military unit. Many have flattened the organization, having limited or no middle management. Many new organizations have less rigid reporting structures. "Manager-less" is a term some companies have moved to. They might have people who coach team members but without a reporting connection.

Technology teams may sometimes try out new things as they have with new software engineering methodology during the Agile Revolution. I am sure that in ten or fifteen years, the technology we use and the structure of the team working on it will be quite different. Keep an open mind to what comes next. If you don't, you might be pushed out of the industry.

IT Titles, Departments, and More

I am always amazed while talking to people who don't understand what goes on in Information Technology or IT. Most people who have never worked in this department believe it just includes developers and help-desk technicians. Of course, they usually hold a few stereotypes about us as well.

Architecture

Architecture plays a misunderstood role in technology. People in this department try to develop systems at a high level. This can be quite challenging, so people with some experience are usually preferred in these positions.

Infrastructure

The system that everyone wants to work on but no one knows the location of: infrastructure. This might include devices in a server room or perhaps machines on the cloud. Wherever they might be, someone has to manage them and keep the infrastructure running.

Network

We connect to all of these things over the network which is much more than just Wi-Fi. Most people connect to the network and want to make sure it works well. The network is the vital backbone of commerce today. If computers were unable to connect to outside networks, we would not be able to interact with other systems and share information.

Devices

When I first started working in the technology sector, smartphones didn't exist; I know, I am a dinosaur. Now, the devices that we can use to access organizational systems are amazing. We can now work from almost everywhere. While this is certainly an advantage, it can also be a curse.

Security

The overarching move towards more connected devices has pushed security to the forefront. Organizations are keeping a closer eye on information, websites and applications. From the barrage of news about data leaks of large organizations' information, we've learned how important this is.

Software Development

A steady push to teach more people to code has developed and the demand seems to continually increase as we become more reliant on software. Developers come in many flavors and specialties. From old mainframe systems to new mobile platforms: organizations need them. While working as a developer for almost twenty years, I have seen many changes, but the demand is still there.

DevOps

Mixing operations and developers is great for tackling some of the challenging changes asked of technology teams. This is a relatively recent phenomenon that seems to be gaining steam. The idea is that when these two roles are brought together, they can collaborate and solve problems quickly.

Testing and QA

I like to get things done quickly, yet I also know I if I get in too much of a hurry I may miss things. Having a solid quality assurance team has saved my bacon many times. Testing is a real art and most programmers don't do it well. Even if they perform test-driven development, they often focus on the wrong things.

Program and Project Management

Project management has encountered a substantial change as more organizations embrace agile project management. The traditional waterfall method is used less and less. We have learned a great deal about how difficult it is to estimate time. Employees work better when tasks are assigned in small chunks and feedback is provided.

Business Analysis

Understanding the business is very valuable. I have worked with some wonderful business analysts that understand the process and procedures well. Creating software without the assistance of someone who really understands can be quite problematic. They need to be detail-oriented and patient to work with developers.

Requirements Management

A phenomenon that is common for IT projects is "scope creep", otherwise known as requirements management. I find this process similar to how my teenage son keeps asking for things after my wife announces she is going to the store. When an analyst or product owner begins to gather requirements, they must perform a litmus test, deciding what is in and what is out.

Process Engineering

Handling consulting for large companies, I've found they have the process nailed down. Maybe too much for my liking sometimes, but they probably need it. Large companies usually have a process for changes that must be followed and sometimes this consists of a review board. This can be helpful as organizations grow and more people become involved.

Business Intelligence and Reporting

Technology departments are asked to report on many things. When they are required to deal with large amounts of data, analyzing it properly can be difficult. Due to the recent explosion in big data, i.e., data sets that are too large or complex for traditional data-processing application software to adequately deal with, more companies are researching data they have already collected from their applications and systems to understand how they can use it. They rely on their data and reports to guide intelligent decisions.

UX

Effective User Experience, commonly referred to as "UX", has become critical to application success. I confess to having poor design skills related to user interface and experience. An intuitive layout allows people to jump in and start using an application quickly. If the layout is cumbersome, a user manual needs to be created. This can be a good sign that changes need to be made. Applications by companies that do this well can gain wide adoption.

Finding the Right Fit for You

Technology teams do not consist only of developers. It takes many different types of employees to make technology work and change as desired. A full complement of skills and styles is needed to make everything work together. Let's discuss a few aspects involved with finding your place within the team.

Depth

If we quickly jump into technology, it can feel like we landed in the deep end of the pool. Parts of it may be challenging and hard to understand. I suggest that you allow yourself to be challenged or you will find yourself becoming bored quickly. It may take time to find the right depth for you.

Possibilities

The list of careers within technology continues to grow and grow. As new technologies emerge, more roles are created. If you find yourself not feeling connected at one organization, it is important to realize that you may need to try a new role. Look for a new challenge that may fit you better.

Technical Breadth

Technology professionals know their specialty well. What many of them struggle with is seeing how the whole operation works together. Similar to how a great orchestra conductor appreciates the importance of each instrument, having a high-level understanding of each part of an operation is essential. I approach most things by trying to gain a big-picture view first, while I realize that many may approach things in a different manner. You don't have to know exactly how a watch works to tell time with it. For a technologist, seeing the big picture can be a challenge.

Synergy

When we look at the big picture of technology, we can see many connections. Even between an old technology, Cobol programming, and a new technology, the Internet of Things (IoT), there are connections. Today's push to create a hub for home automation is similar to the push for mainframes of old which were the central hubs of technology in most companies. With a small amount of digging, we can find ways that technologies may complement each other.

People Management

Confronted with all the bits and data, we sometimes forget what is really at the heart of the matter: people that work together and make things happen. People management is still required; there is no app for that! Disagreements over data and output continue to occur, of course. So, don't leave your people skills at the door.

Coaching and Mentoring

Coaching and mentoring are often considered interchangeable. This is a mistake as they are indeed different. Coaching is targeted assistance or reflection on a particular topic. When I was starting my business, a business coach helped guide me with getting things off the ground. Mentoring is more inclusive and discussions can be on many topics. Mentoring is based on the relationship between you and your mentor.

Care and Support

Individuals need different forms of care and support. A few years ago, I led a team consisting of people that were quite different from each other. Some were newly out of college and needed a lot of guidance while others were more experienced than me. They all just needed support and freedom to do their work. Managing people well is a skill that takes time to learn. As you gain experience, you will understand the various kinds of care and support that are needed.

Logic and Rules vs. Creativity

Software engineers are drawn to logic and rules and they try to find order in a random world. I once worked with a guy named Duke who would attempt to make everything around him ordered and logical. He even insisted that everything at his desk stayed in a certain order. One thing out of place and he would become irritated. In contrast, designers who tend to be more creative look at the world differently. They see shades and many colors where engineers see everything in black and white.

Tools or Systems vs. Applications

There are many ways to organize a technology department. Like drawers in a kitchen, each organization goes about it differently. Some may organize the department around tools or systems while others might arrange it by applications. This can lead to interesting specializations that people pursue in their career. One application may require those who know the .Net Framework and SQL to make changes. Other organizations might segregate the work into development and database work.

More than a Paycheck: Salary and Benefits

Technology has long been a sector that pays well. With higher pay, though, comes pressure to perform and solve some challenging problems. Each company may compensate in various ways. Some companies essentially offer salaries where others offer stock options and additional benefits. One could say that comparing compensation is complicated.

<u>Salary</u>

Those of us who work for a straight salary mostly have full-time employee positions. Overall experience will have a major effect on this. Your skills and their demand are additional factors. Certain types of developers can demand a higher salary and expect to get it.

<u>Stock Options</u>

Technology people occasionally do goofy things for positions with stock options. Some see this as a chance for a great financial windfall. Many startups dangle this incentive to get people on board, yet statistics tell us that startups rarely succeed.

Established companies that provide stock options generally don't grow at an upward trajectory.

Benefits

Depending on which stage of life you are at, benefits may excite you. Some companies provide their employees with meals daily or a few times per week. If you are focused on growing your retirement portfolio, you may be interested in a 401(k) plan and other savings vehicles.

Team

Basketball fans know that Kevin Durant joined the Golden State Warriors last year. While the team was already a great team, he made them even better. Professionally, you might be fortunate enough to find a great team to join. Like Durant, you might be willing to accept a lower salary to work with exceptional people. If you're looking to join a company that is growing quickly, you might accept a role or position that doesn't necessarily best suit you. Deciding which criteria work for you is important.

Timing

I wish I could claim to have learned patience over the years. Unfortunately, I cannot. This lack of patience has burned me in relation to hiring decisions. Previously, when I was wanting to add someone to our team, I hired a less than desirable candidate.

Keep this in mind when you are looking for a position as well. Make sure you don't act too hastily. Ken, an old friend of mine, jumped ship too quickly to leave a bad position, then found he'd moved to a position that was even worse.

Contracting

Contracting can be appealing because although there is safety as a full-time employee, working as a contractor provides a financial incentive. The gap between full-time salaries and contracting work is approximately 30% annually, according to Mike Stanfel from Global Tech Services. Check with technical staffing professionals in your area to gain a better understanding. Employment markets can fluctuate quickly. Of course, it's important to understand the added risk as it is easier to be let go when you are contracting. Companies are much more likely to let contractors go before laying off full-time employees. Contractors must ensure their skills are marketable given the additional volatility.

Startups

We would all love to have careers like Steve Jobs and Steve Wozniak: build something small and start a huge company. Unfortunately, many startups don't turn out this way. Odds are against becoming huge. Although starting a new company might pay off eventually, I would consider it for other reasons as well. If you have a new idea that most companies won't touch or in a developing industry, make the decision to go forward without looking for a big payday. Too many aspiring entrepreneurs make bad decisions expecting a huge return.

Part II - Operation and Engineering Issues

Understanding Business Stakeholders

"Your pain is the breaking of the shell that encloses your understanding." - Khalil Gibran

When speaking to coworkers who have younger children, I often think about my experiences as a parent. Having two kids of my own, we have a shared understanding and empathy. Going through our children's many stages presents great challenges and opportunities for learning.

In business, similar shared experiences can be observed. Organizations grow and shrink while they make many changes. Gaining a basic understanding of what people do and need can help us develop empathy and relate to their struggles. Before I was in software, I worked in sales and this experience helped me understand things that someone without that experience might not be able to grasp.

Common Issues

While working in the software development arena for many years, I have run into some issues common to those faced by others in the business. You will no doubt receive similar feedback from teams you collaborate with.

A sage old developer I once worked with said, "Everything is easy to those who don't have to do it." Often, when he was second-guessed by managers, he would try to explain all the steps involved in a current process. They frequently stopped listening after the first two. Working with technology is difficult and problematic. Some days, everything works as expected but other days, the job can be quite frustrating.

Changes

When working with different systems, you may find that configuration can be challenging. If you purchase or begin using a system that quickly achieves 80% application completion, there will be trade-offs. More than likely, you cannot change everything, so the initial development speed that you gain comes at a cost. On the other hand, a solution cannot be completely coded from scratch. Coding from scratch provides more flexibility but can take a lot longer.

Ready?

Before we had iPads for our kids, traveling to grandma's house was a chore, because she lived over three hours away by car. My son would ask repeatedly, "How much longer?" We could not get to grandma's house fast enough. Most teams include someone like this, who always feel the changes they want take too long to materialize. They ask about it at every meeting and in the hallway. You may get to the point that you walk the long way to the breakroom just to avoid them.

Estimates

I have spoken a bit about the #NoEstimates movement in the agile world. The main idea is that we are terrible estimators of time needed to complete work. Instead of estimating, we should break projects into small chunks and iterate the work (repeat the process to completion). The time spent estimating is a form of waste. Of course, that doesn't stop many executives from asking when the feature or application will be done. The mountains of evidence that says that humans don't estimate well doesn't appear to deter them. I recently received an estimate for car repairs at a body shop which caused me to think about the estimates we make in software development. Repairing a fender on a car and re-designing a software system have some similarities. The big difference, though, is the inherent complexities of software design. If you are pressed to provide an estimate of time required or expected cost, you may give one, but chances are that it will be wrong.

ROI

Corporate management can be obsessed with determining the return on investment (ROI) in all aspects. They may try and break down each phase to look at the value. This can be problematic as many times the value is understood only after the culmination of work and effort. Some preliminary work needs to be completed before the team can accomplish all of the objectives. If we focus on only one phase, the complete cycle may be overlooked.

Trimming

Trimming the organizational ranks is a management standby. If a company is publicly traded, a constant demand for performance may exist. A corporate executive in the 80s made his name by trimming the ranks and trying to increase profitability. His nickname was "Chainsaw". Al Dunlap eventually fell into disgrace when his efforts to trim organizations and show good numbers were found to be fraudulent. As a manager, your goal should be to have a productive yet lean team. Realize that you will often be understaffed.

Common Engineer Issues

While working as a software engineer for many years, I have heard many of the following refrains. In fact, I have said many of them as well. It's easy to become fixated on certain issues and complain about them. Growing up in a small town, I've observed that developers are similar to farmers who complain about the weather whenever they meet. If you are not a developer and come across some of them talking shop, they will almost certainly be covering these issues.

We Need These New Tools

A friend of mine used to sell tools to mechanics. He drove a big truck carrying many chrome-plated tools. He told stories about how the auto mechanics would go into debt to pay for their tools. Luckily for developers, they aren't usually expected to pay for their tools. Developers can hold practically religious beliefs about some of their tools. The arguments I have witnessed over my years in the technology field were very intense.

Best Practices

In the business world, sometimes we have to put out code that is not perfect. This can drive some perfectionist developers nuts! I know what this type of person is like because I used to be one. I worried about whether the formatting was completed a certain way and if the right software pattern was used. Just a few weeks ago, I was trying to persuade another developer on this very issue. She wanted to review every line of code from the junior developers. The delays were already substantial, and this was only going to make matters worse. Occasionally, developers need to be reminded that they are working for a business. The bills must be paid before worrying about having pristine software.

Technical Debt

The issue of technical debt is something I have been concerned about many times. Similar to dealing with financial debt, we occasionally have to cut corners technically as well. This type of debt can cause problems in the future when trying to make more changes. While progressing throughout my career, I have learned to look at the longevity of a project. In a computer application that might not last more than a few years, software developers really shouldn't be concerned with technical debt. Now, most employees of an organization don't make enough of an effort to understand the volatility of the organization. A few years ago, I became concerned about technical debt for a project I worked on. A few months later, the organization moved in a different direction and this was no longer a concern.

Excuses

Software development attracts people who can instantly immerse themselves into the details from the start. I can attest to being this sort of person at times. Those who are responsible for completing projects can find excuses to explain why things won't work. Technology can be challenging in many ways. Throughout my technology career, I have learned to focus on the possibilities, not the obstacles. Leaders can certainly be afflicted by this sentiment as well. Somewhat tongue in cheek, some have said that the CIO should be called the CI"No".

Limited Time

Developers only want to release their work when it is perfectly complete. Yet, in their minds, it is never perfect. During my experiences in software development, I have been exposed to the concept of minimum viable product. MVP refers to the technique through which a new product is developed with sufficient features to satisfy early adopters. Championed by Eric Ries in his book, *The Lean Startup*, this idea is used in many business settings today. Getting products into our customers' hands to see what they say is very important. The opinion of people who might pay for the software is quite valuable.

Operations and Security Pitfalls

From an outsider's perspective, information technology operations can seem quite mundane. I once heard someone refer to it as the "feeding and watering of the servers," similar to a rancher who just checks on the cattle. Of course, that's painting a simple picture of it in contrast to real life where operations engineers have a lot of issues to wrestle with.

Security is another challenging position. In a small company, the operations personnel take on security responsibilities too. In larger firms, security is a specialization all its own. During one week of news, you'd very likely see at least one security-hacking story. Big companies are mentioned in the headlines when hackers consider them a big catch. Small firms get hit with security issues as well.

Licensing

Software licensing is confusing even for the people who enforce it. Technicians and administrators often have a difficult time keeping the rules straight. Major companies like Microsoft and Oracle change the policies from time to time. Products change continuously and the cloud creates a new challenge. The old model of sending out updates is gone. This is a new paradigm of storing information in the cloud as opposed to in the computer on your desk. Currently, Microsoft uses Outlook 360 to push their email application to the cloud. The stated goal is to manage applications better by eliminating issues with backups and system upgrades, but we can never be completely sure.

Support

Business owners pay a lot for software licensing in hopes that they can receive support if they need it. That sounds great in theory, although once you begin to use the software; you will invariably run into a gray area. While using numerous paid-for packages, I have been told by software companies, "That is not supported," essentially having my hand slapped. Even worse is finding a suspected bug that you would like fixed, submitting it, and hearing that "the software is working as expected." This would be the perfect place to insert an open source rant, but I choose to move on and cover additional pitfalls.

Policies

Organizations like to establish policies as they grow. Early in my career, I worked for an organization that was small and scrappy. They hadn't instituted hardly any procedures to follow so we just did what needed to be done. We acquired a lot of new business and the company grew. As it grew, things changed. All sorts of rules were added. As a developer, I needed extra memory for my development tools but this didn't comply with the desktop policy. I was forced to get special approval to make this happen.

Approvals

Policies can slow work down, along with process review boards. After a few mishaps, many companies institute a process review board. This is a weekly meeting of employees in different departments where they review any upcoming changes and alert parties to new items. The idea is a good one, but typically, better communication would accomplish the same thing.

Insiders

Security experts know that one of the biggest company threats is insiders. People who you work with have the potential to compromise sensitive information. It might be someone with malicious intent or coworkers who are ignorant of the data they have access to. The next Snowden may be working in your organization. To protect against these threats, proper measures need to be put into place.

Cyber Attacks

As state-sponsored cyberattacks occur with greater frequency, organizations can get caught in the fray. Their systems must be patched and ready for these attacks. It is critical for organizations to monitor advancing standards in protection. The US government is working on establishing standards to thwart these attacks. The possibilities that are coming can't be ignored.

Programmers Be Crazy!

A few years after the movie *Office Space* came out, my brother-in-law told me I had to watch it. "This is your life," he stated, somewhat tongue-in-cheek. Since he is a dentist, he felt he could make fun of those of us who work in offices.

In the movie, Bill Lumbergh, some of the programmers' boss, passively asks the team to do more than they already do. In one exchange, he tells them, "Yeah…I'm gonna need you to come in on Saturday." Then he follows that with, "Oh, and I almost forgot. Ahh, I'm also gonna need you to go ahead and come in on Sunday, too." Managers like this can be hard on developers, but programmers can be tough to work with, too.

IPS

From working with a few irascible programmers, I have found most a bit challenging to deal with. One of my managers used the term "IPS" for irritable programmer syndrome to refer to their personality. Developers can become cantankerous when they are bothered or asked questions. One such developer I worked with was Adam. My co-workers and I would take turns asking him questions to see if he was having a bad day. We joked that he should have a yellow flag taped to him so people would be cautious around him.

Introverts

Not to paint with a broad brush but some programmers don't like to talk. One programmer I worked with, "Edward", was an extreme case. He asked for all requirements to be emailed to him. He refused to attend meetings as well. Until I read Susan Cain's book, *Quiet,* I did not understand this. She explained how most people cater to extroverts to the detriment of introvert friends. Open workspaces and numerous meetings are not good settings for introverts who need different types of environments to thrive.

Denial

Developers are not the most creative people. They are really good at determining why things can't be done. Software developers can be prone to saying no. This gives developers as a group a bad name. The better way to communicate is to offer options. List the different ways the problem can be solved. Also, when offered a tough choice, ask a few more questions. Try to understand what they are getting at.

Tradeoffs

Oddly enough, many developers act in a binary fashion. What I mean by that is they seem to see the world in black and white. They either agree with you or are totally against your request. It's necessary to understand the many options and tradeoffs available. I know I sometimes act this way when I am asked to complete something ahead of schedule. I may just respond with "No". The better decision is to ask questions and detail the tradeoffs. For example, "If you want the TPS report done by Friday, which of my other two priorities should I de-emphasize?" Or, "If we remove the report section, the changes can be completed by Friday; would that be okay?"

Food is Influence

A little-known fact is that if you want influence with developers, you just need to buy them food. A manager who needed some quick changes for her application discovered this when she brought in pizza. After requesting the same changes numerous other times, she'd been ignored. The pizza did the trick. One food item that will gain the most influence over developers is chocolate chip cookies.

Part III - Assets and Branding

It Is Great to Be Here!

"We are lucky to be knowledge workers and in such a healthy industry." - Greg Jensen

The technology sector offers many great jobs to choose from. According to CompTIA, 6.7 million people are currently working in the US technology sector. "A U.S. tech industry worker averages an annual wage of $105,400 compared to $51,600 for the average private sector wage." So, the pay is good and there is a lot of opportunity in the technology arena.

Gratitude

After reading a few books on positive psychology, numerous reasons to practice gratitude are apparent to me. A few Debbie Downers can be found in every line of work, including technology, but overall, this field has many more great things going for it. I am thankful for the countless new things I have learned over the years. I never feel I am doing the same thing for long as something new is never far away.

Square or Role?

Occasionally, while coaching my son's basketball team, we must run a zone defense. For instance, sometimes the team is down a couple players when there have been a few injuries. A zone defense can help make up for poor conditioning or lack of height. This type of situation can happen in technology teams too. Some team members may need to cover for someone who left or is on vacation. When an individual fills a square, he or she may be responsible for many tasks. When a person fills a role, their focus is on one or a few key tasks. In the small organizations I have worked for, the technology team covered a square. There was not enough work for each of us to specialize in certain things. Larger organizations tend to have more specialization; therefore, people fill a role and can become really skilled at it.

Why Are You Here?

In Simon Sinek's popular book, *Start with Why*, he details how leaders can inspire people when they understand why people work where they do and what drives them. Whether we're leaders or not, it is important for us to know why as well. Is your 'why' simply a paycheck? Or is there more in it for you? From working with many different people in technology, I've noticed that some just love the tech. Others appear to be inspired to solve problems. I fall into the second camp. I have always enjoyed a good challenge and like to solve problems big and small. If you feel the need to play with new technologies, that can be a demanding desire. In this fast-paced high-tech world, changes happen quickly. Be sure to know *why* you are here and keep that reason in the front of your mind.

Perfect Job

If the perfect job was created for you, one that would best fit your skills and personality and position you to provide the most value and make great contributions, what would it be? Think about where you are at now. What aspects would you like to change? Do you feel like you are adequately challenged? We need to push ourselves to learn new technologies and skills.

Your Most Valuable Assets

"Half of the troubles of this life can be traced to saying yes too quickly and not saying no soon enough." - Josh Billings

As a middle-aged man, I have learned a few things about how hard I'm able to push myself. While focusing efforts on our job, family, and a few side pursuits, we also need to take care of our most valuable assets: our body and mind. Pushing too hard over long periods of time may cause problems. I am not afraid of hustling over a short haul as we all must do that from time to time. When the weeks turn into months with no end in sight, however, something has to give.

Essentialism

Michael Hyatt turned me on to the idea of essentialism in one of his older podcasts ("The disciplined pursuit of less"). Between overscheduled lives and too many responsibilities, we need to simplify our lives. I've found the idea intriguing and helpful as we all often struggle with too much. Recently, I listened again to the audiobook, *Essentialism: The Disciplined Pursuit of Less* by Greg McKeown. Periodic reminders of having too much going on are something I need. If you haven't read it, I definitely recommend that you do.

Self-care

As a father of two teenagers, I've seen them eat food that would give me a stomachache. My son loves Zombie Burger's, "The Walking Ched," for which the buns are replaced with macaroni and cheese. Part of taking care of yourself is eating good food for fuel and staying hydrated. Eat too many cheeseburgers and your energy will start to diminish. Sleep is also an important restorative activity. Don't try to burn the candle at both ends for too long or you will pay the price. I find that daily exercise helps me keep focused for longer periods of time. Without it, I feel sluggish.

Time Management

When you work at a full-time job, you need to manage more than just your work. For instance, 32 hours might be budgeted for the job each week. But along with that, 3-4 hours of time should be set aside to communicate with your co-workers and manager as well as to manage co-workers and expectations. In the technology sector, it is also important to continue learning and studying best practices. In an average week, I recommend spending 4 hours reading and researching. Then add a few hours for networking with other professionals at your company and from other companies. I find user groups to be a great networking resource. For instance, when I lived in Central Iowa, I attended the Central Iowa Java Users Group, Des Moines Area Quality Assurance Association, and a few other user groups to stay connected with the technology professionals in the area.

Quality of Life

As a kid, I became aware of a few workaholics; most prominently, my father. He worked as a farmer and would push himself quite hard. People in technology can drive themselves hard too. This takes its toll and can cause weight gain and loss of family by focusing too much on the chosen career. Take time for your family. Whether you are married or single, build those relationships. Develop friendships and hobbies outside of work. Take time to grow in other realms. A few of my co-workers are also musicians. and have found that taking the time to learn something new or practice a current skill or hobby relieves stress.

Protect your most valuable assets. Look at all the things you do and discover the essential elements. Care for your mind and body and take time to live a meaningful life with friends and family. Your work and life will become more rewarding by having balance.

Building Your Personal Brand

"The keys to brand success are self-definition, transparency, authenticity, and accountability." - Simon Mainwaring

We each have a personal brand. Some of us work on building it while others may simply let it progress on its own. Becoming aware of the various parts that make up your personal brand is very valuable. Most of my technology friends have ignored this fact. To really stand out, though, working to make a brand that is exceptional is vital.

Authenticity

Never try to be someone you are not. As you build your personal brand, be sure it is authentic. Oscar Wilde advised, "Be yourself; everyone else is already taken." While you may want to imitate a famous tech titan, it is best to be yourself.

Performance

Recently, co-workers and I tried a new restaurant. We were quite impressed with both the staff and the food. A few weeks later, we decided to return. The next visit was completely different. This time, the restaurant service was slow, and the quality of the food was poor. Similar to a restaurant's brand, how you perform is part of your brand. Focus on making it consistent. Take pride in the work you do, day after day. The hallmark of a true professional is performing their job well, day in and day out.

LinkedIn

Technology people tend to move around between companies more than in many other industries. In light of this, having a LinkedIn profile is important. Essentially, a profile on this platform begins with your online resume. Then you can add connections and recommendations. Of course, some people avoid it as it's common for many recruiters to contact you. Frequent contact by recruiters is not always a bad thing as they can be helpful when you are looking for a new opportunity.

Community

Being part of the community is always advantageous. Technology communities can be quite tight-knit. Working in Des Moines for almost twenty years, I am always amazed at the strong community. Even though Des Moines is not a major market, we have many strong technology groups. Our local .Net developers group (https://www.meetup.com/iadnug) and Agile Iowa learning community (http://www.agileiowa.org) are quite strong. Each one holds yearly conferences that draw huge crowds. One great way to build your brand is to get involved with your local community.

Participation

A few years ago, I became involved in a group. I reluctantly began to serve as an officer in the group. In retrospect, I realize what a great opportunity it was to participate and give back. I helped the small group grow and transition into a larger group with more involved members. We all think we are too busy to be involved, but I would recommend trying it out. You will learn more than you can imagine. Plus, you may discover something that you excel at in the process.

Permission

Building your brand means you must create a unique one. Don't create a brand by copying someone else's ideas that you don't have permission to copy. This frequently happens online when people find someone else's great design and decide to copy it. Also, organizations have guidelines for what you can share and how you can share it. For instance, if your company is acquiring another company, some information sharing likely requires permission.

Just Ask

One excellent way to understand your personal brand is to ask other people. Ask them what they think your brand is. You might receive some surprising responses. If you don't like what you hear, perhaps you have some work to do. Find others who have a stronger brand. Look at how they created the brand; likely you will learn some lessons from this.

It Is All in the Performance

"How you do anything is how you do everything." – *Unknown*

As a big sports fan, I know how important performance is. I wish I could say the Chicago Bears football team has impressed me, yet their performance this year has been lacking. I am honestly rooting for a good draft pick at this point. Sports remind us how important results are. Granted, some sports athletes have resorted to cheating, but I am not advising you to do that. As technical professionals, we also need to keep an eye on the results.

Results = Performance

The phrase "results matter" is often repeated. Even when we intend to do the right thing, we all are judged mainly by our results. The outcome is so important. Early on in my management career, I became more aware of my responsibility for the team. Our team missed some key results and I took the fall for it. Because the team did not perform as expected, I was let go. the team's performance was my results as a leader.

Consistency

The saying, "How you do anything is how you do everything" is difficult to attribute. Perhaps it was originally a Buddhist expression or spoken by someone not well known. Regardless, it is important to realize that what we do and how we do it matters. I wrote this book between Christmas and New Year's, a time when most of us would like to take it easy. But we still need to put in the same effort towards our work, despite anything that might distract us. Every day counts if you *make* it count. Consistency will strengthen your performance.

Improvement

Your employer wants you to continually improve at what you do as this makes the company more productive. Hopefully you want to do the same. Sure, we would all like to make the small change that creates a great positive impact on production, but this rarely happens. Instead, look for opportunities for small improvements along the way, like the flywheel that Darren Hardy talks about in his book, *The Compound Effect*. As we make small changes, the flywheel slowly starts turning. Over time, the momentum builds, and we see big changes.

Feedback

I recently listened to the Manager Tools "Basics" podcasts (https://www.manager-tools.com). Multiple episodes focus on feedback. Managers find that feedback is important to help people perform at a high level. In my experience, people tend to give feedback sporadically. High performers need frequent feedback. Don't wait until it's review time to share advice, because by then, it may be too late. Also, be sure the feedback is prompt. Time it so that changes can be made and time isn't wasted.

Growth

Great performers constantly add new skills as they don't want their careers to stagnate. Look for opportunities for growth. One simple way is through audiobooks. I am able to access numerous books from my local library with a simple app on my smartphone. The next time you run to the grocery store or commute to work, you could be learning something new. Look for new skills to add or improve on current skills. Try out this new time-management technique to save time.

Communication

Technology workers have often gotten a bad rap and are known for being poor communicators. We tend to leave things out of the conversation. After explaining something once, we still may think that it was one time too many. This has a big effect on our performance. As with many things in technology, these effects are often not visible. We need to let people know when our work is complete. When tasks dependent on our work remain, we need to make sure the affected people know. They can then finish their part.

Your Online Brand with LinkedIn

When I first graduated from college many years ago, a resume was an important job search tool. Today with the arrival of LinkedIn, it has become relegated to a second-class document. Using LinkedIn to capture your career snapshot, accomplishments, and connections appears easier. However, I still run into people who don't have an account or have an orphaned account.

Resume

Do we need resumes anymore? I am sure you could make a case for not creating one, but I would recommend keeping one up to date along with your LinkedIn profile. For the most part, I think they should mirror each other. The resume should be more concise. LinkedIn is an online resource so you can share more there. In the future, it's possible no one will have resumes, but let's keep one around for a little longer.

Hiding out

In technology, I have met a few people who abstain from LinkedIn. The reason I've heard most often from these people is that they don't want headhunters contacting them. Having a wonderful LinkedIn profile through which placement agencies cannot connect with you is possible. A few of my tech brethren can, be shall we say, introverted. They don't care to talk to anyone who doesn't grok (understand) code. This can spell disaster when they are looking for a new job. Have something on LinkedIn and elsewhere online. Don't be like Luke Skywalker hiding out on Ahch-To.

Update

As with your resume, keep your LinkedIn profile up to date. I am not sure why, but some people are afraid to change their profiles. As you learn new skills, make sure to add them to your profile, as well as any new co-workers. You never know who might be able to connect you to a position that better fits you. In addition, as you gain a few years of experience, it's easy to forget some of the technologies and projects you have worked on in the past.

Search

Take some time to browse people's profiles to find out what they've included. Doing so will help guide you when deciding what information to add to yours. Frequently, I coach people to spruce things up and make their profile professional. LinkedIn changes and evolves, so what works today won't necessarily work in a few months or years. Experimenting with changes is very helpful. A friend who does consulting made some minor tweaks to her profile and soon received a lot of business.

Photo

Always post an updated professional photo. I like to have fun as much as anyone, but your profile photo needs to convey some professionalism. Along with a good profile photo, add a nice background photo that fits your industry. Both will help build your brand so make sure they are high-quality images.

Summary

Create an effective but concise summary. Don't try to cram too much into it either. When you create the summary, use keywords that relate to your work and industry. For instance, developers can include languages they use or are proficient in. Keywords will make your profile stand out when employers are searching for candidates.

Passport

Think of your profile as a passport instead of narrative. It can transport you to the next stop on your career journey. As you explore new career options, a LinkedIn profile can open doors. Connect with people who can assist you along your path.

Branding Through the Community

"Communication leads to community, that is, to understanding, intimacy and mutual valuing." - Rollo May

Our brand is built by the community we create and affect. Groups we join and participate in, whether formally or informally, are part of our brand. As a youth, one of my friends made some poor choices. This reflected on me as I was grouped with him and some others. To change my brand, I had to change my associates.

Communities

I am currently working with two coaching clients. One client has really embraced the developer community. He is involved in some user groups and has a strong network. The other client has been hiding out and pretty much keeps to himself. I am sure you would be able to guess who has the better prospects for employment.

You Inc.

We are each a company to ourselves. If you work for an employer and receive a salary, your company (you) has only one customer (also you). Or perhaps you run your own business and work periodically for many clients. Some people can handle the entrepreneur mindset while others need more security. I should point out, though, that the security some people feel they need is really more of an *illusion* of security. A company can change quickly, possibly forcing you to find a new employer.

Customers

How do you treat your customers? You might be wondering, "What customers?" If you don't sell anything, you likely think you don't have any. This type of thinking can be dangerous. If you view co-workers or clients as more of a nuisance than customers, you probably treat them poorly. Technology work is primarily service work. We either help clients—if working as a consultant—a company, or complete tasks to serve their business goals. Think about this the next time you want to snap at someone. Take a deep breath and remember who you serve.

Helpfulness

In West Des Moines, a local grocery store, Hy-Vee, has a slogan that declares, "We have a helpful smile in every aisle." I am not suggesting that you plaster a fake smile on your face. Only that you remember to be helpful. Keep a positive tone and communicate thoughtfully. Don't let your emotions get the best of you.

Muscle Memory

Don't do your work well because people might forget your good work; do it well to guarantee you won't forget how you did it, through exercising your muscle memory. Remember the habits you create are important. "Excellence is an art won by training and habituation. We do not act rightly because we have virtue or excellence, but we rather have those because we have acted rightly. We are what we repeatedly do. Excellence, then, is not an act but a habit." This quote from Aristotle highlights how we need to mind our habits and use our muscle memory wisely. To put it another way, sometimes we *should* sweat the small stuff.

Part IV - Mindset and Culture

Participate and Share

"Participation, I think, [is] one of the best methods of educating."
- Tom Glazer

Children in preschool and kindergarten spend a lot of time learning how to share. Depending on the size of each child's family, this can be easier for some and harder for others. older. By the time I came along, my older brother by five years thought he was in charge. He didn't want to share. My younger brother came along a year later, so, I don't remember not wanting to share. Simple lessons like this one can often show up in our work as well. Once, I noticed someone's shirt that said, "Doesn't play well with others." Unfortunately, many professionals encountered should display this warning.

Participation

Technology tasks require people to work together. Participation is more the rule than the exception. Recently, I was troubleshooting an issue with a co-worker. We were both confused and needed some additional help. With some additional expertise, we were able to come to a solution. Look for opportunities to participate in group discussions. Chances are, if someone invited you to join, they value your opinion.

Sharing

My son used to play hockey. While watching practice, I would often talk to a gentleman who owned a detailing business. He spoke about how busy he was and that he couldn't keep up with all the work. I asked him why he didn't hire someone to work with him. He replied, "I don't want to share all my secrets." He worried they could leave and start their own shop. That type of thinking is quite dangerous in technology. In truth, when you train new people, you bring value to the organization. Sharing your expertise helps you as well. Helping others grows your influence and grows the organization as well. Too many people have a small mindset and look at everything as a zero-sum game, where there must always be a winner and a loser. Another important aspect of technology is that it changes so fast and no one can know everything. There will come a time when you need others to share with you.

Introverts

Working in technology for almost twenty years, I have encountered a few introverts. Getting them to share can be quite difficult. In *Quiet* by Susan Cain, she describes how to work with introverts. One important way is to give them space and time to think. Acknowledge them in your groups and allow them to write down their idea or to share by other means. Try to organize the workplace so they have quiet spaces to concentrate.

Extroverts

You never have to ask an extrovert for their opinion: they will just blurt it out. They also tend to dominate the conversation. It's necessary to help them learn to allow others to share. Start with subtle cues and then move to more direct responses. Try to determine whether you are more often introverted or extroverted. Also, become aware of situations in which you may be prone to be one or the other.

Honest Efforts

Making an honest effort to find ways to participate is important. Identify your strengths and try to make use of your skills to help others. My wife shared a great question that would be useful to ask when attempting to assist others. She suggested that a co-worker should start a meeting and asked her, "How can I help you out?" That is an excellent, direct way to show you can help.

People connect when you are genuine. Show your vulnerability and come out of your shell. A few people I have worked with seemed pretty stiff. It can be challenging to relate to people who present a facade all the time. As a coach, I honestly express to people that I am not perfect and many times I learn from them as well.

Your Story

Make sure you share your story with people. Let them know where you come from. This can help you connect with them and discover their story too. Don't try to be someone you're not. Part of your story should include both wins and losses. People won't believe you if you only talk about your successes.

Permission to Succeed

"When your self-worth goes up, your net worth goes up with it." - Mark Victor Hansen

I am sure you have met people whose success you thought was a sure thing. In the movie, *Moneyball*, Billy Beane is called a "can't-miss prospect". As the story unfolds, Billy is perplexed by this situation. Yet, he becomes a general manager of an MLB team and tries to learn and understand why he had great potential but didn't live up to it. He learns why he had failed and how he could use the information for evaluating baseball prospects by focusing on key statistics. People often overlook their mental beliefs in their success, as it starts there but takes work to build true success.

<u>Permission</u>

In Earl Nightingale's classic, *The Strangest Secret*, he talks about the need to believe in ourselves. Many of us sabotage our own chances of success. You may feel you are not worthy of success, so start by giving yourself permission to succeed. Don't think about all the reasons you can't succeed but think of all the reasons why you should.

It starts with you. No one is going to approach you to tell you to succeed. The decision comes from inside. Once you believe in it, then you can make it happen. This principle is similar to an important aspect of sales. If a company or salesperson doesn't believe in their product first, no one will buy it. The product you are selling is you. If you don't believe in yourself, you are going to run into a lot of trouble.

Assessment

Take an honest look at yourself. Examine key characteristics and skills and rank yourself on a scale from 1 – 10 in those areas. Remember that people you know will rarely rank you higher than you will rank yourself. This can provide insight into what you feel your weaknesses are. Review this with some close friends and see if you are a tough grader or right on. One thing to keep in mind is that it's common to assess your own skills relative to people you know and work with. If you have worked with some elite people in your field, you might anchor your assessment to this high level. On the other hand, if you have worked with some poor performers, you might believe you rank above average when you are, in fact, just an average performer.

Mindset

We are often our own toughest critics. Some may achieve something but never enjoy it. How deserving of success do you feel you are? Do you perhaps focus on small things you've done wrong, even though you are actually doing wonderful work? These types of comparisons usually take you to a bad spot mentally. Take stock of all you have accomplished and realize the strides you've made. Choose the right mindset.

Belief in yourself is where permission to succeed begins. If your mindset is to think, "I will just try this out," the outcome will only be mediocre. There is nothing cornier than expressions by the character Yoda. But one of his most famous, "Do. Or do not. There is no try," seems to encapsulate how critical our mindset is. Some may view confidence as arrogance but building that internal confidence is necessary. Expect success during your attempts and don't become irritated if they don't work out. Develop a quiet confidence, not only learning from setbacks but also expecting to eventually triumph.

Don't Be Bashful, Just Ask!

"Successful people are always looking for opportunities to help others. Unsuccessful people are always asking, 'What's in it for me?'" - Brian Tracy

In some situations, I don't want to bother someone by asking a question. Many of us can be bashful at times. If we follow that thinking, however, we will usually miss out on opportunities. It can never hurt to ask. The worst thing that can happen is that they say "No." As I started my own business, I realized this lesson. Many years ago, I worked in sales, and an important aspect of lack of success in this arena related to hesitation to ask questions.

<u>Just Ask</u>

Asking for a favor or guidance is really this easy. We simply need to ask. Don't put a lot of thought into it; that is when our rationalization skills kick into gear. *I don't want to be rude*; *I don't want to be all 'salesee'! I don't want to...* Stop yourself right there then ask what you need to ask. In the fall of 2018, I organized the Agile Online Summit. To execute successfully, I had to ask a lot of people for help and favors. Most of the time they were willing, and sometimes not; that was okay. Just because a few aren't interested in getting involved in your project, doesn't mean you shouldn't do it.

This principle is universally acceptable. Don't just apply it with your close friends. Recently, I was talking with two gentlemen who had started a successful startup company. Their relationship had begun when one of them asked to be introduced to the other. Their initial meeting progressed to a budding relationship, then to business partners. All from asking for an introduction. Who should you approach next?

Obstacles

Randy Pausch shared his last lecture at Carnegie Mellon University in 2007. He had been recently diagnosed with pancreatic cancer and was told he had a few months to live. He shared a lot of great wisdom with his students. One particular piece was about obstacles. He spoke of brick walls that "give us a chance to show how badly we want something." Mentally, we often let our fear of asking someone a question become an obstacle. If your life depended on it, would you change your mind?

Pressure

Don't pressure people into feeling obligated to help you. Ask without expectations. Simply ask for a favor and if they can help you out, great. But if not, then don't consider it a big deal. Some people are interested in helping others and some are not. Their interest or willingness may depend on their position or your relationship, as well.

The same principle applies when people ask you for help. If you can help them out, by all means, do so. Clarify their request so you understand what they are asking and be sure you can deliver what they want. If you can't, can send them to someone who can, if possible. Be a resource that is willing to share connections.

Whatever you may need, throughout the course of your career, don't forget to ask. The simple act of asking could open doors for you. It could also enable you to help someone else who needs guidance. Whether a small or large favor, make an effort; the worst that could happen would be for them to they say no.

Evolving Your Mindset

"Your mindset matters. It affects everything – from the business and investment decisions you make, to the way you raise your children, to your stress levels and overall well-being." - Peter Diamandis

I have not always agreed with this statement. In the past, I couldn't really see how mindset would make a difference. I also did not realize that I was living with the scarcity mindset. Scarcity mindset is the belief that our skills are fixed and we can't improve them. In the words of Michael Hyatt, I was "playing small." Because I lacked confidence, I was not achieving what I capable of.

Evolving

To understand this, I needed to evolve my mindset. A simple choice we must make is either to complain and criticize, or grow stronger and happier. This is not easy nor quick to do; I am still working on this. Occasionally, I lapse back into the scarcity mentality.

Core Values

Nobody reminds us to define our core values as well as the late Stephen Covey. In *7 Habits of Highly Effective People*, he described how we should start to work on our character ethics first. The first three habits mentioned focus on creating true integrity with our thoughts and actions. By defining our core values and creating our mission statement we can set our bedrock principles.

Collaboration

Work to foster a culture of open and honest collaboration. An open dialog can generate ideas and opportunities. Look for ways to can help out those you work with through collaboration. Honest feedback is beneficial. Make sure it is constructive and not directed at the person. Avoid attacking people personally.

Mindset

Carol Dweck's work on mindset has been eye-opening for me. She conducted some amazing research and discussed it in her book *Mindset: The New Psychology of Success*. Dweck provides instruction about how to think differently about ourselves and how we raise our children. Characteristics we thought were-set from birth, we now know are flexible. Using the growth mindset, we can learn and grow. The fixed mindset believes the opposite, that we have what we have and it doesn't change. Your thoughts determine who you are.

Imposter Syndrome

At the Agile Online Summit, Billie Schuttpelz spoke about the phenomenon known as Imposter Syndrome. It seems perplexing that people who have accomplished so much can still feel they are a fraud. Or that people who are perfectionists can be overcome by this fear and compare themselves with an impossible standard.

Above the Line

Practice keeping your mind 'above the line' when it comes to responsibility and accountability (*see Chapter* "Staying Above the Line: Drama or Presence"). Don't let 'below the line' beliefs permeate your culture. Look out for lack of respect and withholding of ideas. These negative trends can start small and snowball to destroy the strong culture that's been established.

Developing Your Own Tech Radar

One of my friends sells investments for a large firm and used to send me an investment newsletter. Each month, the company's analysts would put out recommendations to buy, sell, or hold certain investments. They color coded them green for buy, yellow for hold, and red for sell, modelled after a stop sign to advise what to do. If only a sign like this was available for all technologies encountered.

Eureka!

A few years ago, I worked for a company that sent all of their developers to the local *No Fluff Just Stuff* conference. At this event, I listened to Neal Ford explain how to create our own personal technology radar. Considering the countless technologies out there for us to learn, I thought this was a helpful way to filter choices.

Tech Radar

Neal broke up the concept of tech radar into four quadrants: techniques, tools, platforms, and languages & frameworks. Depending on your role, you may want to alter some of them. If my role was as a database administrator, I could swap out a couple of these functions for similar ones. From there, he introduced rings: the outermost representing 'hold', then 'assess' and 'trial', and the inside of the ring represented 'adopt'. This idea can apply to individuals, teams, or companies. Of course, you could modify the rings in other ways as well. One company chose to create a remove ring. They would use this idea to guide removal of technologies from their stack.

Update

As technologies change and evolve, this radar needs to be updated. The area of numerous cloud offerings can change rapidly. Another evolving area that could affect your business is cryptocurrency. Set a schedule to re-visit this topic and reevaluate what is new and what needs to go.

Groups

In a post on his website (http://nealford.com), Neal discussed how to create tech radar for a group. Using sticky notes, you could brainstorm different items and break them down into the four quadrants. Then the facilitator can help group things in each quadrant. Next, the group can discuss the merits of why some should be moved to either the adopt or trial quadrant. One of the most important parts of this process is the discussion. As a group, it's important to derive a consensus on how to move forward with these items.

Adoption

Understanding the innovation adoption lifecycle is critical. Depending on your background, you may not have been exposed to it. Ford further describes this lifecycle curve and I believe it can be quite helpful with understanding types of customers. I studied this concept in college as well. The cycle starts with a small slice of customers, the innovators. Then the early adopters and early majority of customers are in the next part of the lifecycle. As the lifecycle curve begins to diminish, adoption by the late majority and the laggards groups of customers occurs. Think about some of the technologies you currently use. Where do they fit on the lifecycle curve?

I have seen a lot of changes in technology over the years. The exercise of determining your own personal technology radar would be quite beneficial for those working in the technology sector. In the process of coaching professionals, I am constantly amazed at how some have allowed their skills to stagnate. I enjoy learning new skills; yet have noticed that many of my colleagues do not routinely challenge themselves to learn new things.

Defining Your Core Values

"One of my core values is diversity of everything." - Brad Feld

The idea of core values is thrown around a lot. Companies share what their core values are. Politicians talk about theirs. Individually, many of us won't take the time to define our core values. At times, I have been slow to say no to things that are outside of my core values. In high school and college, I made some decisions that I needed to backtrack from quickly. Once I started to establish my core values, I was able to say no to the wrong things and yes to the right things.

Alignment

In our professional lives, we need to identify work that fits our core values. For instance, if you find yourself working at a company that asks you to do something that violates your morals or the law. How you handle this situation can be a big question of alignment. Luckily for me, I have not yet run into a major misalignment like that. Without core values, we won't know if we are getting off track.

I have run into a smaller scale alignment issue when I worked for a company that allowed a team member to treat his teammates poorly. This situation helped me understand it was time to move on. This was the final step toward helping me see how I wanted to be treated and how I wanted my teammates treated as well. Define your core values and you will be better equipped.

Clear Communications

The value of clear communication is obvious but still deserves mention. Honest, clear communication can seem old-fashioned to some. People who have ulterior motives may try to appear honest but their communication will seem incongruent. Communicate your intent and be honest with those you work with. Don't play games with your co-workers or team.

Ownership

Take ownership of your career and professional life. When coaching my son's basketball team, I often find myself stating that the team needs to beat the other team and the referees. In our work life, we may make the mistake of similarly concluding that every setback is caused by our boss or company. Yet, your career is your career. No one else is responsible for it.

Craftsmanship

After working as a software developer for a few years, a co-worker mentioned the book, *The Pragmatic Programmer*. In the book, Hunt and Thomas compared software developers to carpenters or craftsmen. They discussed how necessary it is to learn to use all available tools. At the time, I had learned a few tools as a developer. After reading that book, I realized how much I still needed to learn. To be a true craftsman takes time and experience. In software development, experience is essential too.

Recognition

We all want to be recognized for our contributions. Fortunately, there are many ways to show thanks for your team's work. As a software developer, I felt that on the whole, developers were not recognized enough. There work is really accomplished behind the scenes, and not in the forefront. As a leader, I try to acknowledge each team member's work. It often is best if we recognize the entire team together. Individual recognition can get tricky as some people may resent unequal recognition or at least recognition *perceived* as unequal.

Customer-centric

Technology professionals can become confused about what is most important. Many of us went into technology because—wait for it—we like technology! Geeking out on technology is not a bad thing, but it can be problematic when we think it is the *only* thing. In reality, the customer is the most important thing. Everyone in business should develop customer empathy. Observe their frustrations and why they need us. Focus on the right thing.

Dogfooding

Some of the best products in the world were designed by people who realized a need for them in their own life. I recently read an article about a mother who designed an ingenious device to keep her child's things together. A product's users can understand why it's necessary and the problem it solves. When a company uses its own product, this is called "eating your own dogfood." Beware of companies who don't engage in this practice. They have lost the customer-centric approach.

Results over Politics

Throughout my professional career, I have tried to avoid the drama and politics. Honestly, I naively thought that approach would work for most companies. However, a few people that I've worked with liked to play games and would pit people against each other. Some leaders seemed to think this type of competition will bring out an employee's best. This type of drama can actually wreck a team and drive people to leave. As a leader, I make an effort to focus on results and admit when I make a mistake.

What Do I Look for in Culture?

"Culture is the arts elevated to a set of beliefs." - Thomas Wolfe

In Tony Hsieh's book, *Delivering Happiness*, he discusses how he discovered the importance of culture. When he founded his first company, Link Exchange, he hired people that he eventually regretted hiring. This caused a great deal of stress when he finally sold the company to Microsoft.

Collaboration

Growing up as one of three brothers, everything was a competition for us. We raced through almost everything we did. As my career grew, I found that collaboration was more helpful than competition. Look for a culture that inspires collaboration as open and honest collaboration encourages fresh ideas.

Diversity

Living in Des Moines, I've noticed that Iowans often think it is not a diverse community. Working in technology for almost twenty years has taught me a lot about different countries and their cultures. Between work and travel, I have observed more cultures than I thought I ever would. Diversity is important for allowing people to safely share ideas and challenge existing norms. Technology workers can be sharp and want to think differently than most people around them.

Judgement

Tom Hanks's performance in the 1994 film, *Forrest Gump*, was quite memorable. Especially so as my wife and I went to see it on our first date. The character he played, Forrest, so plainly spoke a phrase that has been repeated frequently, "Stupid is as stupid does." We are usually judged by our actions. People may surmise someone is not too bright by some things that person attempts. As an adolescent teen, I did a few things that likely sent the wrong message. In business and our careers, perhaps we also need to think a bit before acting.

Links in the Chain

The people you work with deserve your respect. Remember, it is highly unlikely that a single employee is smarter than the rest of their co-workers combine. Don't be too hard on a teammate that makes a mistake. Chances are that you will experience highs and lows as well. Look for ways to build each other up and share the credit whenever you can.

Failure

One strategy I've found enlightening when used during a job interview is to ask about company failure. An organization that is realistic will acknowledge they have had many failures. Some companies try to hide them. Chances are that those companies are not places you would want to work. Look for organizations that talk openly about failure. Innovative companies try many things and know that every plan or action is not guaranteed to work.

Are You Looking for Abundance or Scarcity?

"No matter what your ability is, effort is what ignites that ability and turns it into accomplishment." - Carol Dweck

<u>Potential and Growth</u>

As an avid reader, I see multiple applications for material in certain books. One of these books is Carol Dweck's book, *Mindset: The New Psychology of Success.* Her work has really shattered a lot of assumptions many of us held dear. As a young man, I was praised for being smart. Dweck details how this can actually be quite problematic and lead to susceptibility to the "curse of potential."

The potential for greatness seems like such a great thing on the surface. When we are praised for intelligence and the potential we have, the fixed mindset is established. This idea suggests that we have a fixed ability that won't change, no matter how much effort we put forward. Dweck explains how she previously thought this way until some kids who solved puzzles helped her discover a new way to think about it.

In a research study Dweck conducted, jigsaw puzzles were offered to participating children in two groups. When asked whether they wanted to try a more difficult jigsaw puzzle, children in one group replied, "No". This was the fixed mindset group who believed their skills were static. Children in a different group liked challenges and believed they could get better at solving puzzles. This was the growth mindset group.

Choice

In *Mindset*, Dweck explained how we all have a choice to make. We have the agency to decide how we view ourselves. How a person views themselves can have an impact on how well they change and learn new things. One example of a fixed mindset that she shared was John McEnroe. His famous tirades occurred when he knew he wasn't going to win. He would blame everyone but himself. In contrast, Michael Jordan displayed a growth mindset. As his career progressed, he learned new skills. For example, he developed his outside shot and defensive skills.

Words

The words we use also influence how we view ourselves. The mindset you embrace can determine whether you try to face new challenges or cling to the old adage, "You can't teach an old dog new tricks." The words we use also affect those we work with and our families. Dweck discussed how important it is to praise children's effort as opposed to their intelligence. Work and effort are key parts of the growth mindset.

If this concept is new to you, I suggest you check out the Khan Academy video, "The Growth Mindset" which provides a really good introduction. This approach applies to so many facets of our lives; try it out in one area, then keep expanding.

Are You Real or an Impostor?

"I am not a writer. I've been fooling myself and other people." - John Steinbeck

If John Steinbeck suffered from impostor syndrome, then we are all in good company! After working in technology for almost twenty years, one would think that I feel confident about my skills and expertise. As technologies come and go, we can quickly feel our skills become antiquated. Our minds may work overtime at sabotaging our success or accolades we have received.

Confidence

Do you feel confident? Or do you feel that confidence slipping away? Professionals in all lines of work can suffer from impostor syndrome. If you are new at something, yet confident, perhaps you're naive. Doing something for a few years should instill confidence. Doubt can find ways to creep into your mind.

Impostor Syndrome

What is impostor syndrome anyway? According to an article in *Psychology Today* ("The imposter syndrome"), this term refers to "high-achieving individuals marked by an inability to internalize their accomplishments and a persistent fear of being exposed as a 'fraud'". So, if you have become afflicted with this, then you are not alone. We need to stifle our internal critics and realize that we are *not* frauds.

Overcome

If we feel as Steinbeck did, that we are fooling others, we also think we will eventually be discovered and exposed for the frauds we are. As a coach, I try to help people understand they can be successful, but they must give themselves permission first. That sounds silly, doesn't it? Yet, this is the truth for many people who sabotage their own success and believe the myth that they are impostors.

While facing this challenge, we need to find ways to overcome it. An article by Gill Corkindale in *Harvard Business Review* details steps for how to deal with the undesirable consequences.

Rewrite, Reframe and Visualize

What story do you tell yourself? Pay attention to your self-talk and focus on making it positive. Begin telling a new story about yourself. We will always have doubts, but it's important to change our story. At first, this seemed silly to me; then I began to work on this and noticed beneficial changes.

Reframe failure as a learning opportunity. Reveal the lessons and use them constructively in the future. This is a critical message for everyone. I recently read John Maxwell's *Failing Forward*. In his book, he shares how many of the greats have become successful simply by failing *more*. Don't be afraid of failure: lean into it!

In a story about Walt Disney, someone remarked to his wife at the opening of Walt Disney World what a shame it was that he couldn't see his park completed because he had died shortly before the park opened. Walt's wife explained that it was not a shame at all as Walt had imagined the whole thing in his mind first. He was, in fact, the first person to see it all in his vision of the park. In the same way, we must visualize our own success before we can make it happen. Expect success instead of listening to our "impostor" brain. Keep the doubters quiet!

Staying Above the Line: Drama or Presence

Greg Jensen and I have been collaborating for a while. We presented last fall at Iowa Code Camp and are working together for Iowa Business Analyst Development Day (IBADD) too. In a recent discussion, he explained the concept "staying above the line" from the book *The 15 Commitments of Conscious Leadership*.

The book explains how as conscious leaders, we need to understand whether we are working "from presence or from the drama triangle". Presence is above the line and the drama triangle is below. Most organizations spend the bulk of their time in the drama triangle. Here is where people focus on blame, being right, and fear.

Character Roles

The drama triangle consists of three characters. The "Hero" is focused on providing temporary relief, not facing the real issues involved. The "Villain" attempts to lay blame on others, using statements such as, "You should have..." and "It is *your* fault." The third character is the "Victim". They focus on dealing with problems caused by others, and the effects. A person, circumstance, or condition is the root of their problem and the victim in the drama triangle is powerless.

When we move above the line, working from presence, these characters change. The "Victim" becomes the "Creator" and takes responsibility for their lives. The "Villain" becomes the "Challenger" and applies healthy pressure that leads to breakthroughs. Finally, the "Hero" becomes the "Coach" and empowers others to create their desired outcome. Teams that work above the line are more energized and aligned with each other.

Statements of Commitment

Let's examine a few statements to help you understand the differences between both attitudes.

Is this statement above or below the line?

I commit to taking full responsibility for the circumstances of my life at My Current Job, and I commit to supporting others to take full responsibility for their lives.

How about this one?

I commit to blaming others and myself for what is wrong at My Current Job. I commit to my role as a victim, villain, or hero and take more or less than 100% responsibility.

What do you think about these next two sets of statements?

I commit to growing in self-awareness. I commit to regarding every interaction as an opportunity to learn. I commit to curiosity as a path to rapid learning.

I commit to being right and to viewing this situation as something that is happening to me. I commit to being defensive, especially when I am certain I am right.

Did you notice the different tones in each set?

When you find yourself stressed, try the following approach:

Breathe, Pause, and Shift. Become aware that you have drifted below the line and commit to leading and interacting with others from a place of openness.

Part V - Leadership

Stepping to the Front

"Leadership is practiced not so much in words as in attitude and in actions." - Harold S. Geneen

I was naive about leadership for a long time. I thought there was only one type of leadership: when someone granted you the title of leader. Recently, while listening to a Manager Tools podcast, three types of leadership were discussed. The type I previously spoke of is positional power. The leadership type that results from having a great relationship with someone who then helps you out is relational power. The third type is expertise power and is experienced when you are an expert on something which causes others to listen to your opinion and act on it.

Providing Leadership

Anyone qualified can provide leadership even if they don't have the title to go with. Whether it is for a group of friends, family or an organization, leadership is necessary. Start by leading yourself in a manner that others want to follow. From there you can grow your leadership skills. Learn to provide leadership and you will develop a skill that is transferable to every position.

Leadership Significance

Lately, a trend has developed of discussing how organizations can essentially operate without leaders. Many technology companies have claimed they can do this. This situation reminds me of some professional sports teams whose coaches are essentially figureheads leaving the team without leadership. When a strong leader comes along, they can have a significant impact and change the team for the better. Phil Jackson had this effect on the Chicago Bulls and Los Angeles Lakers. Both teams already had superstars but were not winning teams. Once Phil's leadership entered the picture, performance improved dramatically.

Knowledge of Leadership

Ideally, one should know a lot about leadership before becoming a leader. This is why I recommend that everyone learn some basic leadership principles. While studying leadership, I became aware of the many types of leaders we could choose to develop as and leadership skills we could endeavor to acquire. To help with your selection, one simple exercise is to think about the leaders you have worked with. What have you observed that worked well? What would you say is a sign of bad leadership? Develop your own point of view on leadership.

Leadership Ecosystem

Whatever organization you work for, your role will change. Perhaps in small, subtle ways or in more obvious ways. You may gain influence as you become the expert on a new project or receive a promotion to team leader. The role you begin with will evolve within the company. These experiences help you grasp how dynamic the industry is.

Quick Wins

Any time a new leader comes on board, people watch their performance. As an incoming leader, finding tasks or projects you can accomplish quickly to achieve some quick wins will help. Give your team something to talk about and they will share it with everyone. Other leaders and teams will take note that you are putting points on the board and not wasting any time.

Build the Team

Once a house is built, it usually doesn't require very much additional work. Teams are different in that they require constant building and tweaking. Team culture is more like a garden that needs watering and weeding. Ensure that positive ideas and habits are taking root. Follow up by encouraging the right behaviors.

Leader Performance = Team Performance

"Management is about human beings. Its task is to make people capable of joint performance, to make their strengths effective and their weaknesses irrelevant." - Peter F. Drucker

Recently, I listened to Shawn Achor's *The Happiness Advantage*. In it, he talks about the mirror neurons that we all possess; if we see someone smiling, these neurons cause us to be drawn to smile as well. He goes on to relate this to how a leader's outlook towards work is reflected in their team. Leaders can take the team to new heights or to record lows. Influence can be directed either way in both work and home settings. Let's talk about how a leader's outlook can affect the team's performance.

Task Focused

Leaders and contributors may become overly focused on tasks. When we've accomplished everything set before us, we feel a sense of relief. If we aren't able to, we become frustrated. The first thing to do is ask two questions: Does this task need to be done at all? Non-important and non-essential tasks frequently find their way into a list or plan. Does this task need to be done *right now*? Perhaps this is an important task that can be completed later or by someone else.

People Focused

Required tasks are important, but leaders must focus on their people first. Leaders are responsible for driving results and developing their people. If they do the latter, the former takes care of itself. Make sure your people have what they need. Give them goals and the necessary tools and get out of their way. Support people by helping them become the best version of themselves.

Leader Performance

Are you a leader? If so, how would you rate your level of performance? Leadership performance can be a cloudy item to measure. Dependent on what your team does, you should know your key performance indicators (KPI). If you lead a team of developers, your KPI might be the number of stories completed per interval. Your rating might include an element for developing your team and producing more. Are you building a cohesive team or individual contributors?

Team Performance

The team will reflect their leader. When the leader pushes for top results, the team will follow. If the leader doesn't work too hard and goes through the motions, doing as little work possible, the team will put forth a similar effort. When the leader asks the team for extra effort, they need to step up their game. I have heard a story about a leader who canceled team members' time off and then left for a vacation. This type of mixed messaging can disenfranchise a team.

A leader's performance can be the basis for the team's performance. Leaders should be in tune with their team and understand what obstacles they might be facing. Work to develop your team. Try new ways to bring them together and strengthen their bonds. One reason for poor performance could be toxic team members. This situation can be dangerous and ruin a good team fast. Be alert for this tendency during the hiring process. If you currently have one on board, look for ways to move them out of the team.

Building a Great Tech Team

"Coming together is a beginning. Keeping together is progress. Working together is success." - Henry Ford

Recruiting the right people is not an easy task. Top technical talent essentially have their pick of positions. Companies try to bring in good people, but typically, a few duds will sneak in. Hiring a new person can be tough on so many levels. Even after asking them behavioral questions and grilling them over particular technologies, we can still end up hiring the wrong person. Part of the issue involves rushing to bring in new people. To find and hire the best person for the position, we need to slow down and take our time. Many will protest, "But by then, the good ones will be gone!" That may happen yet hiring the wrong person can be very expensive and can also ruin a good team.

Culture Fit

A truly great team is not a group of rock stars. A great team knows how to work together and play their respective roles. During the 2018 NCAA men's basketball tournament, a 'Cinderella team' advanced to the Final Four. Loyola University Chicago's team beat many higher-ranked teams to reach this point in the tournament. This team did not consist of only top recruits, but they played well together which made the difference.

Similar things happen with great tech teams. When a good culture and talented people who want to work together are cultivated, the bar is raised. Each member helps push the other team members. They learn from each other and respect each other's opinions. Organizations that establish this culture and know what they are looking for consistently find the right people to add to their teams. Organizations that hire flashy candidates or hire too quickly can wind up with some poor fits.

One incompatible teammate can sour a team quickly. Previously, I worked with Cindy (not her real name) for a short while. When we went to lunch on her first day, she complained about a few things. I have to admit, that immediately raised a red flag for me. On someone's first day, most would expect their conversation to be all positive. Cindy was hard on both her teammates and customers. After a short stay, she was let go. Talent is desired, but no one wants to hire talented jerks!

Holding Out for the Right Talent

Feeling rushed is common. "We need someone yesterday!" is a familiar plea. At times, you may even have thought, "Someone is better than no one." Remember, one bad hire can have a net negative impact, as demonstrated by Cindy's example. I've observed from working with developers for many years that one poor hire can create a mess in a hurry. It is best to wait and hold out for the right person.

Dave Ramsey and his organization are notoriously slow in hiring. On their podcast, EntreLeadership, they've detailed the numerous rounds of interviews they send prospects through. Only someone who really wants to work for him will stick it out. I would recommend creating a process and fine-tuning it. If you later discover a crazy one got through, it is time to change the process.

Seed, Feed, and Weed

Let's assume you have completed all of the previous steps: now you're done, right? Wrong! Once you have created your superior team, you still have some work to do. Seed: Constantly be on the lookout for new people. It's likely you will need to grow your team in the future, or someone may leave. Feed: Develop the people currently on your team. Provide the coaching and training they need as one of them may replace you someday. Weed: Some may fool you during the hiring process while others may change. If any become negative or are no longer a good fit, move them out with care.

About the Authors

Greg Jensen is the VP of Engineering at CDS Global, a Hearst company that provides media fulfillment for many marquis media brands in the US and Europe, where he leads architecture, development and delivery of next generation digital experience, commerce and order management systems. Greg has previously held senior technical and executive positions for companies such as AT&T, Best Buy, Dish Network, Lockheed Martin, and Verizon and led multiple startups as a VP of Engineering or CTO. Greg holds a BS degree in Computer Science from Park University and an MS degree in Software Engineering from the University of Minnesota where he also served as an adjunct faculty member at the Software Engineering Center teaching a graduate course on big data strategies and data science. Greg and his wife Patty currently live in downtown Des Moines. linkedin.com/in/gcjensen

Tom Henricksen is a technology professional, career coach, and speaker. He has worked in various roles in technology for over fifteen years. Tom has developed successful technical careers as a career coach for almost five years. He and his wife Jessica currently live in Washington Crossing, Pennsylvania. linkedin.com/in/tomhenricksen

www.ingramcontent.com/pod-product-compliance
Lightning Source LLC
Chambersburg PA
CBHW021836170526
45157CB00007B/2816